T]

A Modern Bible Commentary

BookCaps Study Guides

(An Imprint of Golgotha Press)

www.bookcaps.com

Table of Contents

About BookCaps Bible Commentaries

BookCaps Bible Commentaries are non-denomination study guides for people who are just getting into the Bible for the first time, or who just want to know a little more.

Each commentary, looks at the historical context behind the book, the themes, who wrote them., and study questions. A chapter summary of each chapter of the book is also included.

To find out more about this series and other BookCaps books, visit: BookCaps.com.

Introduction

When one tries to get a drink from a fire hydrant, it is almost impossible because of the volume of water. The book of Mark is a fire hydrant of information from its very beginning to the end of the story. The author knows that something has happened on earth that will change the way people live forever and modify the relationship that man has with his God. The quicker man starts the learning process, the better off he will be.

The fact that God exists is not the news that Mark brings to the believers as everyone knew that God existed. The truth the author wants everyone to realize is the fact that God is here this very moment seeking to be part of the life of every individual on the planet. Mark wants to get right to the point of the story and give everyone the details of what transpired in order that people could live in reality and not in some dream world.

The Author of the Book of Mark

In dealing with any literature of the far past, it is very difficult to ascribe to any one particular person the authorship of a book written some fifty years after the death of Jesus. The same can be said for the book of Mark. Most people believe that the book was written by a young man named John Mark. This individual was not one of the original disciples. John Mark was one of the seventy that Jesus sent out, on an early mission journey.

Very few scholars believe that the book was written by some unknown author, but there is reason to believe that Mark is no more than a redactor of the traditions which were available to him. He wanted to guide and edify his readers. Some people believe that the book of Mark is a product of several different writers and thus a product of the Christian Community. (H.N. Roskam, 2004). There is ample reason to believe that Mark knew both Peter and Paul and he was adept at putting their words into written form. He had heard these great preachers time and again preach about Jesus and what were expected of all believers. The flow of the book indicates that Mark had a great deal to say to the people, and he wrote down all that he had knowledge of in an effort to persuade people to become believers. Nothing is known about Mark's education, but he had to have been a good scribe with a good memory.

Mark is known to be the son of a Mary who had a house in Jerusalem that served as a meeting house for believers. Mark preserved the preaching of Paul and Peter as accurately as could be done and scholars are pretty sure that recorded it correctly. He also appeared as a helper of Paul and Barnabas. Mark and Paul had a parting of ways for a time, but were united again in Rome. Mark and Barnabas made their way to Cyprus for a time just before being reunited with Paul in Rome.

Tradition has it that the book of Mark was written in Rome to the Romans. Mark was in Rome with Peter during Peter's last days. A considerable amount of explanation of Jewish customs is made in the book. From that fact, it is figured that the ones to whom the book was written had little knowledge of the Jewish People and their customs.

One of the ideas that have come to the front of modern thought is the fact that Mark might have been writing in such a manner as to dissociate Jesus and his followers from any form of Jewish nationalism. As the crucifixion is noted in Mark, there seems to be a bit less blame place on the Romans and a considerable amount forced onto the Jewish leadership. As Mark was written to the Romans, one could even think that Mark was trying to convince Rome of his nonpolitical nature. This might be a stretch for some believers to accept, but anything is possible.

Something else that needs to be considered in the study of Mark is the fact that throughout the book there appears to be some sort of special relationship that had been established between Mark and the people to whom he was writing. The way Mark is written might suggest that it was a type of letter to the believers in various gatherings throughout the country. There isn't any way to prove this statement and it really does not matter in the study of Mark.

Nothing is mentioned about the death of Mark. The last time he is mentioned in the Bible is in Acts and from there he just disappeared from the story. Some scholars believe that he was a married man, and he returned to live out his life in Jerusalem. Again there is not any record of this, so one is free to believe as he wishes.

An interesting thought is promoted by many Bible scholars that it was John Mark who fled from the garden the night that Jesus was arrested, losing his outer garment on the way. There are various dates given for the writing of Mark, but the vast majority of the Bible scholars put the date at around A. D. 55. Some learned people believe that the book was written as late as A.D. 65. It is also agreed that the book was written before the destruction of the Temple in A.D. 70.

Historical Background of Mark

The book of Mark is really nothing more than the story of Jesus Christ. It is not meant to be a history book nor will it detail everything that was happening in the world at the time. The book concentrates on Jesus and the things he did while on earth. As with any book on a particular subject, special reason existed for the writing of the work. In the case, of Mark, Jesus and his way of life are the central focus of the story. The book of Mark really lends itself to the oral tradition as it can be told in a very story-like fashion and in small segments that really displays the life of Jesus.

As with the history of all of the gospels, what is important is the condition of the people, at the time the book was written. Unlike the book of Matthew, Mark was written for the gentiles of the day by a practicing Jew. Scattered throughout the book are small explanations about Jewish tradition, written so that the gentiles could understand what Mark was telling them. There is little doubt that the book was written before all of the other gospels and was probably penned in the late A.D. 50's.

The world of that time was very much like the world of the later gospels. The same places existed as they did in the book of Matthew. Jerusalem was a very busy place at the time of Mark and was a central trading center where traders supplied the merchants of the city with goods from all over the world. The Roman army had a cohort stationed in and around the city which contributed to the hard currency supply of the city. The farming in the area also provided the farm produce that the city needed as well as a little surplus that the farmer could sell for hard currency. The economics of the time were not really that bad. Life was hard but not unbearable. The Roman taxes fell hard on the people but again they did have the hard currency to comply with the Roman system.

The Jews were still looking for the Messiah who would come and free them from the Roman yoke. They were looking for a military leader who would field an army and drive the Romans out. Little did the Jews know but the army that was to be created was not an army of swords and spears but one of love and service, an army that could not be defeated by the might of the Roman Empire. There was a group of fighting Jews that were constantly under arms and attacked the Romans at every turn. The Zealots never had the power to defeat the Romans, but they continued to be a thorn in the side of Roman government.

At the time of Mark, Peter, and Paul, Galilee was the original home of Christianity. It was in Galilee that Jesus worked most of his miracles and from Galilee that he called the first disciples. Jesus made his home in Capernaum which fulfilled a prophesy in Is. 9:1-2. (F. J. Foakes-Jackson, 1927). Josephus devotes two sections of his book on the Wars of the Jews to the area around the lake which shows how important he considered the area. One of the things that the Jews hated was the fact that Herod Antipas built the city of Tiberias at the site of an ancient cemetery. (Josephus Wars III: 10.7-8.)

The area where Jesus started his ministry was thickly populated by the Jews and the Greco-Roman Gentiles. Galilee was evidently in a prosperous condition, and considering everything else, it was well governed. At the time of Jesus, the area was pretty much at peace. In the time of Mark, the first great rumblings of the revolution were starting to be heard in the Jewish camps. One thing that can be said about the Jews of Galilee is that they were a much simpler people than those of Judaea. The Jews of Jerusalem were a hardy and courageous lot which the Zealots exploited and prompted the destruction of Jerusalem.

The Purpose of the Book

In the early years of Biblical study, the book of Mark did not receive very much attention. It wasn't until the nineteenth century that interest was developed in the gospel. The search for the historical Jesus prompted the scholars to visit the book of Mark. It wasn't too long before they decided that the book was really the most reliable source of the knowledge of Jesus. (H.N. Roskam, 2004). History shows us that the early believers were a persecuted people. They had no friends among their Jewish brothers nor did they have any peace with the Romans.

Written language allows people to communicate with the past. The gospels are classics much like the Odyssey and the other great literature of the time. The Jews were devoted people who considered every letter of the Torah as sacred. With the coming of Jesus, believers gave birth to an entirely new movement that impacted all of Western civilization to a greater extent than any other form of writing. The Bible comes from the past, but, as believers read it, it is interpreted in the present time. The scriptures are passed from one generation to the next with basically no changes made in the source material. It is through history that believers seek to understand the past through a study of the Bible, where the believer's source of Jesus is found.

When looking at the New Testament books of Matthew and Luke, it is discovered that they have borrowed over two hundred scriptures from Mark. It can be said that Mark is the oldest of the gospels, but there is a possibility that Mark had access to some related stories that were older than his story. There is a certain amount of artificial linking of the various stories and the historical sequence of the events in Mark may not be in the correct sequence. (Schuyler Brown, 1993).

Mark was written to jolt the people of the world into knowledge of how the real world of Mark's time was in direct conflict with the world that Jesus preached about to all who would listen. Mark really allows the reader to see where he or she is in relation to walking with God. It can be surmised that Mark did not have a good relationship with the Jews of his time as he had made his stand on the idea of the Messiah and Jesus. He was not really interested in trying to get his message out to whoever would listen and make a choice to follow God.

As Mark is explored, one must remember that there are as many faces of Jesus as there is the variety of people who call him the Son of God. Jesus can be many things. He can be the liberator, an intellectual genius or almost anything else. What believers have been in search of for these many years is the historical Jesus, the man, the Son of God, the Messiah. (http://www.pbs.org/wgbh/pages/frontline/shows/reli gion/jesus/tikkun.html, April 27, 2011).

Even the Jews have been in search of Jesus the Jew but not Jesus the Christian. To most Jews, Jesus was a holy man of God. It is a bit strange that the church and scholars have gotten along without the historical Jesus for centuries. It appears that most people cannot tell one why it is so important to find the man, Jesus. It is this search for the man that leads believers to study and ponder over the book of Mark. In 1906 Albert Schweitzer called Jesus a "stranger and an enigma." (http://www.pbs.org/wgbh/pages/frontline/shows/reli gion/jesus/tikkun.html, April 29, 2011).

In the 1950s and 60s, another search for the man Jesus was begun. The Jesus movement soon took shape and people did their best to place Jesus on the outside of Judaism in the first century. It was finally decided by learned people that Jesus was preaching about the Kingdom of God and what the future would bring. Some people saw that what Jesus had to say was about god and not about himself.

Regardless of how much study is done and how many theories are developed, several things stand the test of time. In the first place, Jesus was and is a Jew. Secondly from the man Jesus springs the Christian church in all of its many flavors.

The latest attempt at finding the man Jesus and finding something to cling to is the Zeitgeist Movement which attempts to separate what they see as fiction from their concept of fact. It is probably a safe be to not place much hope in their success. (http://www.scribd.com/doc/20194708/The-Zeitgeist-Movement-and-the-Historical-Jesus, April 29, 2011).

Writing Structure of Mark

When one looks at the structure of Mark, consideration must be given to the fact that there were many gentiles living in the area of Galilee. Some figures have the population split almost 50/50 between practicing Jews and non-practicing Jews and gentiles. This gives rise to the idea that the book of Mark was probably written in Hebrew/Aramaic before it was ever written in Greek. Many of the followers of Jesus were Gentiles supplemented by a smattering of Jewish converts. (Maurice Casey, 1999).

More recently, the claim of a strong gentile presence in Galilee has been an important component of the argument that Galilee was thoroughly infused with Greco-Roma culture, an argument based largely on archaeological finds. The inhabitants were often of mixed blood and open to foreign influence and were despised by the ethnically pure Judeans to the south. Archaeological finds demonstrates the influence of Greco-Roman culture and reveal that Jewish-Gentile interaction was very common. (Mark A. Chancey, 2002).

An interesting early claim about the structure of Mark was that the gospel was just a condensed version of the book of Matthew. Scholars now recognize that this is not true as Matthew and Luke quoted extensively from what was written in Mark. The book is not really very impressive on its face. (http://www.michaelturton.com/Mark/GMark_intro.ht ml, April 29, 2011). The Greek of the translation is awkward and had to be cleaned up later by other writers. Chronology is of little sense and characters just seem to appear for a few verses and then are gone. The ambiguity of the book has caused some of the early reviewers to refer to those happenings as Markan errors.

When the scholars started studying the book of Mark, they realized that the book gave them the best overall picture of Jesus and his actions on Earth. In reality, the book of Mark is well-done and very complex in its composition. (http://www.michaelturton.com/Mark/GMark_intro.ht ml, April 29, 2011).

Mark has many sources, and that is the reason that as mentioned earlier some people thought that the work was done by different people or what were referred to as the Christian Community. The Tanakh played a big part in the construction of Mark. There are over 150 direct references to the Tanakh in the book of Mark. Also found in the gospel, are references to Elijah, 1 and 2 Kings, 2 Samuel, and Daniel. Some scholars also argue that "Q" is a source for Mark, as well. "Q" refers to the German Quelle and was developed by German scholars to explain how Matthew and Luke have so many verses with close or identical wording.

Themes of Mark

Jesus is the Son of God

Mark does not waste any time telling everyone who Jesus was. In the first chapter, first verse, Mark simply lays it out for all to see. He relates the coming of John to the "voice of one crying in the wilderness" and seeking to prepare for the coming of Jesus. John adds to the clarity of who Jesus is by telling people that he, John is unworthy to unloosen the latchet of the one mightier than he who baptizes with fire. There is no doubt that John knew who Jesus was, and so confessed his position before Jesus and God.

The Healing Power of Jesus

Jesus began his ministry by demonstrating his power over sickness, and the people were amazed. Chapters 1-3 cause considerable concern over how Jesus spoke with authority and demonstrated his true power over the ills of the world. "The evil spirit in Mark 1:24" is another utterance of the possessed man and his confession of who Jesus was. There was more amazement when they saw that Jesus could control the unclean spirits of the world.

A House Divided Cannot Stand

At this particular time, the Jewish leaders began to take great notice of the power of Jesus. In their best effort, they tried to convince people that Jesus was a minion of the devil or Satan. They believed that only Satan could give power to Jesus to cast out demons. Jesus used this accusation to remind people that a house divided cannot stand. This was a direct and frontal assault on the Jewish leadership. The priests were not teaching the law to the people and in so doing were causing dissension among the Jews. He was basically blaming the leadership of making laws that were not of God or for the benefit of the people.

Persecution

As with any fringe group, those who began to believe in what Jesus was teaching found themselves thrown out of the places of worship. By being persecuted, this further reinforced the idea of the weakness of a divided house. The persecution of the believers was sometimes very violent. Some believers were stoned because they followed Jesus and some had to move from their homes and find other places to live. At this particular time, the Romans really were not interested in the squabbles within the Jewish population. This would change over time. The main thing that the Romans were concerned with was the armed resistance that was being raised by some of the more militant Jews.

Man will be Known by What Comes from his Mouth

The Jews had very strict dietary laws which involved what could be eaten, and the washing of hands before eating. In following the laws that were made by man, the Jews were forgetting the law given to them by God. Jesus preached that it was more important for people to consider what was in their hearts and forget about what they were eating. The Jews were trying to remain holy by following the dietary laws and forgetting that what made them unholy was what was coming out of their mouth. Sin begins with the inner intentions of the person. People are pure because of what a person's mind dwells upon and the actions of that person.

A Believer is to be a Servant of All

Jesus had a very definite idea about who would be greatest in the kingdom of heaven. In Mark, the author makes it clear that according to Jesus he who would be greatest in heaven must be the servant of all. The disciples really did not have any concept of the kingdom Jesus was talking about. They believed that the kingdom is centered in palaces with thrones. Nobody has to keep up with the Jones. The kingdom is really in the hearts and minds of the believers.

Temptation

As Jesus was tempted in the wilderness by Satan, believers are now being tempted by the same individual. Temptation is whatever is placed in front of one which would lead one to sin. The body of a beautiful lady or a handsome man is a temptation for some as the possibility of improper actions is always present. Excess food, money, power, or anything that would separate one from God is temptation. A married man can admire a beautiful woman providing that evil thoughts do not enter his mind, but he can never debase himself by partaking of the forbidden fruit.

With God, Nothing is Impossible

As the people grew in the knowledge of the law, many questions were raised about who would be able to enter the kingdom. Who would be able to meet all of the laws and be right with God? People began to worry about getting into heaven because Jesus mentioned that it would be hard for the rich to enter heaven. People equated the wealth of an individual with the recognition by God for their goodness. Such is not the case. Wealth is not a blessing from God or a reward for being good. The grace of the Lord is all that is required to enter heaven. By the power of God, nothing is impossible, God saves whom he will.

The Greatest Commandment of All

The leaders of the Temple were fully intent on trapping Jesus in some scriptural mistake. It was natural for the leaders to try to trip Jesus up on the Law and to try to get him to say something that would condemn him before the eyes of the people. As with taxes, Jesus defused the question by simply stating the most powerful of the Ten Commandments. We are to love the Lord our God with all of our heart, soul, strength, and mind. Nothing in this world is to be put before God.

The Covenant

At the appointed time, Jesus will be seen in the clouds. Great power and glory will be part of the return of Jesus. From all over the world, the elect of God will be gathered unto Jesus. No man on this earth knows the mind of God and nobody knows when the end of times will happen. In this day, there are preachers on the radio and television who say they know. These people are false prophets as it says in the Bible only God knows. Do not spend much time listening to a preacher who appears to have a direct line to God, at the exclusion of everyone else.

Chapter Summaries

Mark 1

Unlike Matthew and Luke, Mark begins his story of Jesus with a quote from Isaiah the ancient prophet. The scripture he used related to the people that someone was to come to announce the coming of the Messiah. The messenger would come from the desert and be unlike anyone the people had ever seen.John was certainly that, clothed in camel hair and eating locusts and wild honey. Jesus came to John at the Jordan River, seeking to be baptized. When he was baptized ,and came forth from the water, the heavens were parted and the Spirit, like a dove descended to him and a voice from heaven said, "Thou art my beloved Son, in whom I am well pleased." The Spirit then led Jesus to the wilderness for forty days. During this time, he was tempted by Satan. At the end, of the time of temptation the angels came and ministered to Jesus.

John was arrested and put into jail. Jesus came to Galilee preaching, and it was here beside the Sea of Galilee that he called his first two disciples, Simon and Andrew. A little further along, Jesus saw James and his brother John and they also followed him. As Jesus taught, he taught with authority and not as one of the scribes. In Capernaum, they found a demon possessed man in the synagogue. The demon recognized Jesus and Jesus rebuked him and ordered him out of the man. Everyone was amazed at the power that Jesus had. Jesus healed Simon's mother-in-law. News spread about the the power of Jesus throughout the town, and the sick were brought to him. The next morning Jesus and his disciples left so that he could preach in other synagogues throughout Galilee. Jesus healed a leper and told him not to say anything about it, but he could not keep it unto himself and he spread the word about Jesus. More people came to him.

Discussion Questions

The book of Mark is about an individual. Who is this individual?

The prophets of the Old Testament are expressed in the beginning of Mark. Of what importance is "The voice of one crying in the wilderness..."?

How is baptism with water related to repentance that secures the remission of sins?

What allowed John to realize the holiness of his action as it related to the baptism of Jesus?

Explain how the opening of the heavens allows for a unique relationship to be established between God and his chosen people.

Of what importance is the temptation of Jesus, in the wilderness?

What would prompt four men to lay aside their work and family and follow a man they did not even know?

Mark presents a series of events that would demonstrate the unique power of God to a people who were prone to disbelief. What allowed Jesus to witness to the almighty power of God?

Mark 2

Though Jesus continued healing the sick, he began to preach about the remission of sins. It was at this point in his ministry that he really got the attention of the scribes when they heard him tell the man who suffered with palsy that his sins were forgiven. They accused Jesus of blasphemy in that only God could forgive sins. He reminded the scribes that the Son of man had power on earth to forgive sins. At this time, he called Levi to be a disciple. Jesus ate with publicans and sinners and preached to them.The scribes criticized him for eating with those people and Jesus reminded them that the physician served the sick and not the well. He told them that he came to call the sinners to repentance. John's disciples came to him wondering why his disciples did not fast as others did. Jesus reminded them that while the groom was with them, they did not have to fast, but when he left, they would fast. The meaning of the Sabbath was also discussed. Jesus reminded the people that the Sabbath was made for man, and not man for the Sabbath.

Discussion Questions

What is it that now sets Jesus on a collision course with the leadership of the church?

Up to this point, the people Jesus asked to follow him were in a good relationship with the established church. What is accomplished when Jesus calls Matthew or Levi to join his band?

When the term "sinner" is used, what mental picture is formed in your mind about the individual?

Explain, in your own words, what Jesus meant when he expressed the idea that the Sabbath was made for man and not man for the Sabbath.

Mark 3

The Sabbath again came into discussion when Jesus healed on the Sabbath. Jesus tried to bait the scribes by asking if it were right to do good on the Sabbath. The scribes would not comment, and Jesus asked the man with the withered hand to stretch his hand forth and his hand was restored to him. The scribes and Pharisees then took counsel with the Herodians against Jesus and discussed how they might get him destroyed. Jesus then left and went to the sea, followed by a great crowd of people. He asked his disciples to contract a small ship for him lest the crowd overpower him. Jesus continued to heal and preach to all who would follow and listen to him. At this time, Jesus choose the remaining disciples who would follow him. He sent them forth to preach and gave them the power to heal and cast out devils. The crowd continued to press upon Jesus, and the disciples became concerned about him.

The scribes came down from Jerusalem and accused him of being in league with Satan, because the demons obeyed him. Jesus reminded them that a house divided against itself cannot stand. One day, the house would be destroyed, and the house would fall. In essence, Jesus was telling them that it didn't matter what they said about him, but if anyone blasphemed the Holy Ghost, that person will not be forgiven. All sin can be forgiven by God.

Jesus established the family of God. His earthly family came looking for him and stood outside calling to him. The multitude told him that his brothers and mother were outside looking for him, and Jesus asked them who his family was. He reminded the crowd that whosoever would do the work of the Lord is his family.

Discussion Questions

As a Jew, where would you expect Jesus to be on the Sabbath? Why?

The unclean spirits knew who Jesus was. Why would Jesus want them to keep silent about his identity?

Jesus now completes his selection of the last of the twelve disciples. Could there be a relationship between the twelve tribes of Israel and the twelve disciples?

What is your understanding of the unpardonable sin?

Who is the family of God?

Mark 4

Jesus is into his full teaching mode at this point. He climbed into a small boat, and rowed away from the land a bit so he could talk with everyone. He began with the parable of the sower which was a story that made a comparison of something from the daily life of a person to bring life to a spiritual lesson on living. This was the first time that the disciples had been exposed to a parable, and they really did not grasp the meaning of the story until Jesus explained it to them, when they were alone. He reminded them that Satan was working in this world and doing his best to lead people astray. The basic message of the parable was that some would fall away after accepting the word, but others would endure and become of some value to the kingdom.

The parable of the candle explained that when people had the light of the word, they were not to hide it from the world but were to spread their knowledge to the far ends of the earth. The believers must give attention to what they hear and then multiply that by telling others about their experience and their beliefs. Those who hear the gospel must study and help others to learn of God's plan for the world. The gospel will bear fruit regardless of how slowly it starts out.

Jesus further illustrated how the smallest of seeds grows into a might bush. He wanted the disciples and his followers to know that even if they consider their efforts too small in nature, it would still allow the kingdom to grow above what they would expect. The parables also served to create within his disciples the growth that they were to develop. The disciples would remember the parables of Jesus and in their later teachings; they would refer to them in an effort to bring more people into the fellowship.

At this point, the disciples wanted to pass over the sea to the other side of the lake and probably take a little rest from the crowds that were following Jesus. A big storm developed on the lake, and the disciples became very concerned. Jesus was in the back of the ship sleeping and the disciples went to wake him with their fears about what they were facing. Jesus arose and calmed the wind and the sea. Jesus questioned their fear and told them that they must have more faith than they just demonstrated. The disciples were amazed at his ability to calm the storm.

Discussion Questions

What would lead you to listen to the teachings of an individual?

Parables are brief stories, which are intended to teach a spiritual truth. Looking at the Parable of the Sower, explain what is being explained to the people.

If one does not understand what is being presented by the parable, what can be done so that the truth may be made evident?

The size of the beginning effort is not as important as the size of the ending product. All one has to do is look at the mustard seed. It is one of the smallest of seeds, but grows into a mighty bush. What should that say about our relationship with God?

Can fear be a good thing for man to experience?

Mark 5

When the boat reached the other side of the lake in the area of the Cadarenes, they met a man who had an unclean spirit living in him. He was so strong that he could not be bound even with chains. When he saw Jesus he ran to him and the unclean spirit called out to Jesus, and adjured Jesus to not torment him. Jesus immediately called the spirit out of the man. When Jesus inquired of his name, the unclean spirit said that he was called Legion for there were many unclean spirits in the man. Jesus noticed that there was a large flock of swine near, and he sent the demons into the swine and they ran over a cliff and into the sea. Shortly after this, Jairus came to the Lord for his daughter. She was dying and, in fact, had already died. As Jesus was going with him to his home, he was touched by a woman who had been bleeding for twelve years. She believed that all she had to do was touch his garment, and she would be healed. Jesus got to the home of Jairus and bid the young girl to arise, which she did.

Discussion Questions

Explain how it is that the demons and evil spirits knew Jesus, right away, but mankind is still trying to know him.

Give some thought to the fact that Jesus destroyed a herd of swine by allowing the demons to go into their bodies. How can you rationalize his destruction of a person's way of making a living?

How does Jesus demonstrate that the grave has nothing for us to fear?

Mark 6

From the house of Jairus, Jesus left for his own home in Nazareth. He taught in the synagogue, and when the people heard him, they were amazed. They reasoned that this was the same son of the carpenter whose mother was Mary. His own people rejected him, and this sets the stage for him to leave. He could do no mighty works there, except to heal a few people. He continued teaching in the area for a time and he sent out the twelve, two by two, and gave them power over the unclean spirits. He told his disciples to take nothing with them but their staff and to minister to the people. When they were invited in by the citizens, they should stay a bit and then leave. If people did not receive them, they were to shake the dust off their sandals and then move on. The disciples were successful and cast out many demons and healed sick people.

Herod heard about Jesus, and he became afraid that this man was John the Baptist whom he had beheaded. He was afraid that John had come back to torment him. The disciples told Jesus all that had happened to them as they had traveled about the country. Jesus sought to take his disciples away for a time of rest, but the crowd pressed upon him. He preached to the crowd, and it came time for them to eat. His disciples wanted to send them away as they had nothing to feed them. The disciples said that all they had were five little loaves and two fishes. Jesus blessed the food, and at the end of the meal, he had the disciples collect the fragments of the meal. The disciples collected twelve baskets of fragments of the loaves and fishes. Jesus had fed five thousand men.

Jesus commanded his disciples that they were to take a ship, and go to the other side of the lake to Bethsaida and he would go into the mountains to pray. The disciples began to row toward Bethsaida. After awhile, Jesus saw that the wind was against the disciples as they rowed the boat. He began to walk toward them on the water and would have passed them by, but they saw him. They were troubled, and cried out to him and he came to them. He calmed them, and when he got in the boat all of a sudden, they were on the other side of the lake. The disciples were amazed and drew themselves to the shore in the land of Gennesaret. While there, he healed many people.

Discussion Questions

How would you explain the reception that Jesus received in his own country?

From Nazareth, Jesus sent out his disciples and instructed them to take nothing with them and to abide as they are led by the people. If they were not received well, they were to shake the dust from their feet and then move on. Does this have anything to say about what we should do when we tell the story to those who will not listen?

Of what importance is the feeding of the five thousand?

It is believed by some that the disciples still did not realize who Jesus was. They had witnessed the feeding of the five thousand and now they saw Jesus walking on the water and calming the storm. What more could the disciples have wanted to see in order to prove the reality of Jesus as the Son of God?

Mark 7

The Pharisees saw that some of the disciples did not wash their hands before eating which was a violation of tradition. They approached Jesus and asked why the disciples did not wash their hands. Jesus called them hypocrites and said that they honored God with their lips but not with their hearts. Jesus reminded them that it is not what is eaten that defiles man, but what comes from his mouth.Later the disciples asked him what he was teaching, and he told them that what comes into a man passes through and is purged, but that which comes from the mouth of man defile the man because that is from the heart.

At this time, a Greek woman came to Jesus with a daughter who was possessed by an unclean spirit. She wanted Jesus to cast the demon out of her daughter. Jesus responded to her by saying that he came first for the Jews and that they must be saved before anyone else can obtain mercy. The astute woman reminded Jesus that even the dogs under the table were due the scraps from the table. Jesus responded to her and told her to go her way because the devil was gone from her daughter.

Coming to the Sea of Galilee, a man was brought to him with a speech impediment. His friends wanted Jesus to heal him. Jesus healed the man, and his ears were opened and he was able to talk. Jesus wanted the people not to talk about what he had done, but they did. They praised his name and were amazed that he could make the deaf to hear and the dumb to speak.

Discussion Questions

What is it that really defiles man?

What does the conversation between Jesus and the Syrophoenician woman really prove about the presence of Jesus in this world?

Mark 8

Again the number of people coming to listen to Jesus was great. They had nothing to eat and Jesus called his disciples to him and asked them to have compassion on the multitude. Jesus asked the disciples how many loaves they had and was told that there were seven loaves. Jesus commanded the people to sit, and they discovered that they had a few small fish, as well. Jesus blessed the food and the people did eat. When the fragments of the meal were collected, there were seven baskets left over. Jesus sent the crowd away and he, and his disciples entered a boat and went to Dalmanutha.

The Pharisees came to Jesus and began asking for signs that they could believe. Jesus reminded the Pharisees that there would be no sign given other than what he had already done for the people. He and his disciples then left their midst and again went to the other side of the lake. Jesus told the disciples to be aware of the bad leaven of the Pharisees and Herod. The disciples were concerned that they did not have anything but one loaf of bread to share. The disciples failed to realize from the feeding of the two groups of people that Jesus would provide for them.

A blind man was brought to Jesus for healing. He took the blind man by the hand and led him out of the town and then he spit upon the eyes of the blind man and put his hands upon him and asked the man what he saw. The man said that he was able to see men as trees, walking. Jesus put his hands upon him again and asked what he could see. The man's sight was completely restored, and Jesus sent him away telling him not to go into the town nor tell anyone in the town what happened.

At this point, Jesus inquired of his disciples as to who people said that he was. He was told that some believed that he was John the Baptist and others said the he was Elijah or one of the early prophets. Jesus then asked his disciples who they thought that he was. Peter answered for all and mentioned that Jesus was the Christ, and he asked them to not tell anybody of their confession. It was at this time that Jesus first mentioned his coming death. He told them that he would be betrayed, and killed by the government and on the third day, he would rise from the dead and return unto them. Peter rebuked Jesus and Jesus told him to get behind him as he was acting like Satan. Jesus reminded the disciples that they would need to take up the cross of Jesus and take the word into the world, not thinking of their life, but the lives of others.

Discussion Questions

Why are signs or miracles so important for people to see?

It is probably Peter's confession which allows the other disciples to really see who Jesus is. Through this confession, Jesus was now able to start explaining his coming death. Jesus now requires certain things of those who would follow him. What are these things?

Mark 9

One of the things that Jesus said in chapter 9 has confused many people over the years. In Mark 9:1, Jesus told his disciples that some of them would not taste death before they saw the kingdom of God. If taken at face value, one could think that Jesus knew that some of his disciples would see what is referred to as the transfiguration and would, therefore, know that God is real. Peter, James, and John were the disciples whom Jesus took to the mountaintop and who witnessed Jesus talking with Elijah and Moses. A cloud covered them over, and a voice was heard to say that Jesus was his son and encouraged the disciples to listen to him. Jesus bound them to tell nobody before he was raised from the dead.

The disciples did not all experience success as they went on their travels. They actually found a young man that they could not heal. When they approached Jesus about this, he mentioned that this spirit could not be defeated except by prayer and fasting. After this experience, Jesus again told of his coming death and again the disciples did not understand with the exception of Peter, James, and John who could say nothing about what they had seen.

Several disciples were concerned about who would be greatest in the coming kingdom and Jesus reminded them that those who would be great must be the servants of all. He reinforced the fact that the kingdom of God had to be accepted as a child accepts and believes. There were others who did not follow Jesus but were able to do miracles. Jesus reminded the disciples that they were not the only workers for the kingdom.

Discussion Questions

Explain the importance of the transfiguration to Peter, James, and John.

Mark 10

Jesus was again questioned about divorce and how it would be taken care of in heaven. He reminded the people that what God had joined together, man should not put asunder. Jesus blessed the little children and told the disciples to allow the little children to come to him and restrict them not because everyone must enter heaven as a little child.

A rich young ruler came to Jesus wanting to inherit eternal life. Jesus told him what he had to do, and the young ruler told Jesus that he was already doing those things. Jesus told the young man to sell all he had and come follow him. The young man was rich and went away sad as he had many possessions. The disciples began to worry about who could be saved, and Jesus told them that with man it is impossible, but with God all things are possible. Peter was reminded that though the disciples left everything for Jesus they had really lost nothing that would not be replaced over again in heaven.

Jesus again speaks of his death and told the disciples what would happen to him. Again the disciples did not understand what Jesus was talking about, and Jesus had to remind them again that he who would be first must be last. Jesus and the disciples then came to Jericho where they ran into blind Bartimeus who began to call out to Jesus for healing. Jesus wanted to know what he wanted, and Bartimeus told him that he needed to be able to see. Jesus instructed him to go on his way as his faith made him whole. Bartimeus began following Jesus.

Discussion Questions

The leaders of the Jews kept trying to trap Jesus into making statements about laws that the leaders formulated. They tried to get Jesus to acknowledge that adultery did exist. How did Jesus get around their trap?

Again, what is required of a person who would really be a disciple of Jesus?

What was the request of James and John?

What is it that makes a man whole?

Mark 11

Jesus prepared for his arrival in Jerusalem. He sent two disciples into a village to secure a colt that had never been ridden. The colt was found, and returned to Jesus, and it was upon this colt that Jesus entered Jerusalem to the cheers of the people. The disciples and Jesus spent the night in Bethany and in the morning Jesus was hungry. They walked by a fig tree, and as it had no figs, Jesus cursed the tree and his disciples heard it.

The disciples went with Jesus to the Temple, and he began running out the people who bought and sold in the Temple. The scribes and chief priest heard what Jesus was doing and came to the Temple. When evening came, he and his disciples left the city for the country. In the morning, they came by the fig tree that Jesus had cursed and it was all withered. Jesus used the fig tree as an example of prayer for the disciples. He told them if they had the faith, anything they asked would be given to them.

The Temple leaders again came to Jesus and questioned his authority. Jesus turned the tables on the leaders and asked about the baptism of John as to its origination, heaven or of man. The leaders could not answer the question and, as a result, Jesus did not tell them by what authority he did what he did, on a daily basis.

Discussion Questions

Why would the people welcome Jesus to Jerusalem in such a joyous manner?

According to Jesus, what is the lesson of the fig tree?

Mark 12

Jesus related the parable of the wicked husbandmen to all who would listen. The owner of a vineyard sent his servant to his vineyard to get his profit from the crop. His servant was beaten and sent away. The owner sent other people to the husbandmen, and the same thing happened to them. Some of the servants were even killed. He then sent his son to the wicked husbandmen, and they killed the son that they might have the vineyard. Jesus then questioned the people as to what they would do to the husbandmen. The leaders of the Temple knew that the parable was told against them, and they did not question Jesus.

The Pharisees and the Herodians were not done trying to trick Jesus. They asked him if it were legal to pay taxes to Rome. This was done in an effort to get Jesus to talk against Rome and thereby get him arrested. Jesus asked that a coin be brought to him, and he asked who was pictured on the coin. Everyone knew that it was Caesar. Jesus reminded all who would listen that they should give unto Caesar what was Caesar's and unto God that which was God's.

The Sadducees then came unto Jesus asking about the resurrection as they did not believe in the afterlife of a person. Using the marriage argument, they inquired of Jesus if there was an afterlife, and a brother had taken his brother's wife after his death, who would be her husband in heaven. Jesus reminded the people that life in heaven is not like life on earth. There is no such thing as marriage in heaven. He reminded the Sadducees that God was the God of the living and not the God of the dead.

The scribes did their best to trick Jesus as well by asking what the greatest commandment was. Without hesitating, Jesus told them that the greatest commandment was to love the Lord with all of our heart and soul and to love one's neighbors, as well. The scribes reminded Jesus that they already loved like this and Jesus told them that they were not far from being in the kingdom of God. That was the last question that they asked Jesus as they realized that they could not trick him into saying anything that they could pursue to condemn Jesus.

The widow's mite was brought to those who would hear as an example of what true giving was. Many people gave out of their abundance and really gave little. The woman gave all that she had to the Temple and, therefore, gave more than anyone else.

Discussion Questions

What does the parable of the wicked husbandmen mean to the believers?

How does Jesus sidestep the issue of tribute to Caesar?

The Sadducees tried to trap Jesus in asking him to talk about the resurrection. The Sadducees did not believe in the resurrection. How did Jesus disarm their trap?

Explain what the greatest commandment is and how believers are to behave.

Gifts that are brought to the synagogue are really between God and the bringer of the gift. What made the widow's offering greater than any given that day?

Mark 13

Jesus then discussed the end times with those around him. He reminded them that not one stone would be left upon another. Israel would be destroyed. As the Temple would be destroyed, so would Jesus, but on the third day, he would come back to life and would be seen by all around him. The disciples wondered when these things would happen, and Jesus reminded them to not be deceived by false teachers. Jesus told his disciples that the word of God had to be taken into the world so that all could hear it and be saved. The people would be persecuted for what they believed, but the faith would grow, as well. When Jesus is coming back, is not known of men. Only God knows the timing of the Second Coming and no man knows. Jesus told the people that they must always be ready for the Second Coming as even Jesus does not know the time.

Discussion Questions

What must happen in the world before the "end times" come upon mankind?

Mark 14

The Temple leaders began to plot against Jesus seeking a way to put an end to him and his teachings. Judas approached the Temple leaders and told them for a price he would betray Jesus unto them. In the meantime, Jesus and the other disciples were preparing for Passover. All twelve disciples were gathered in the upper room, and, at this time, Jesus told them that one of them was going to betray him. The disciples could not believe it. Jesus told the disciples that upon his rising from the dead, he would go before them into Galilee where he would see them again. Communion was then celebrated for the first time, and Jesus reminded the disciples that anytime they ate this meal, they would be honoring and remembering the servant hood of Jesus. Peter kept saying that he would follow Jesus where he would lead. Jesus reminded him that before the night was over, Peter would deny that he even knew Jesus. After the meal, Jesus took the disciples to Gethsemane where he was going to pray before his arrest. He knew that he was going to do the will of his father even though he asked for the cup to be taken from him. At this time, Judas and the Temple guards came and arrested Jesus. Peter drew his sword and struck one of the Temple guards and cut off his ear.

Jesus was taken to the high priest and the council and was questioned. Jesus held his peace and did not argue with them. The Temple leaders asked him if he were the Son of God and Jesus admitted to it. This really made the priests mad and they began striking him with their hands. Outside Peter made his first denial of knowing Jesus, and before the night was over, he had denied him three times.

Discussion Questions

What do you think caused Judas to betray Jesus?

How did Jesus celebrate this particular Passover differently than in the past?

Like Peter, believers deny Jesus more frequently than they would like to admit. How is this denial accomplished today?

Mark 15

Jesus was taken to Pilate to be judged. The people cried for Barabbas to be released to them and to crucify Jesus. Pilate was taken aback, but so ordered the sentence be carried out. The soldiers took him away and began to scourge him. They mocked him and then led him out to be crucified. The soldiers compelled Simon the Cyrenian to carry the cross of Jesus as Jesus was weak. At Golgotha, they crucified him and placed a sign over him that read "The King of the Jews".

Two thieves were crucified with Jesus to fulfill the prophet's words of him being crucified with common transgressors. People came by and made fun of him by wagging their heads and mocking him by saying that he could save others, but could not save himself. In the ninth hour, he gave up the ghost. The veil in the Temple was ripped from top to bottom exposing the holiest place in the Temple. Joseph of Arimathea came to claim the body, so it could be buried before the Sabbath. A large stone was rolled across the entrance of the cave in order to seal it.

Discussion Questions

Why did Pilate elect to have Jesus crucified?

At the time Jesus died, what supernatural event happened in the Temple?

Mark 16

Upon the passing, of the Sabbath, Mary Magdalene and Mary the mother of James came to the tomb in order to anoint him. They discovered that the stone was rolled away and when they entered the sepulcher they saw a young man sitting there and were afraid. He told the women that Jesus was not there, and he reminded them that Jesus told the disciples that he would go ahead of them to Galilee.

When Jesus had risen, he appeared to Mary Magdalene and to two others who were in the country. The disciples heard what was told to them, but they did not believe what they were hearing. Later Jesus appeared to the eleven as they sat at meat and he chided them about their unbelief. He delivered the Great Commission to them, at this time. After the Lord had spoken to them he was received up into heaven and the right hand of God his father. The disciples then went forth as Jesus had instructed them.

Discussion Questions

To whom did Jesus first appear after his resurrection?

In your own words, what is the Great Commission?

Suggested Readings

H.N. Roskam. (Ed.). (2004). The Purpose of the Gospel of Mark in its Historical and Social Context. Boston: Brill. (Original work published 2004)

Schuyler Brown. (1993). The origins of Christianity: A Historical Introduction to the New Testament. Oxford, UK: Oxford University Press. (Original work published 1993)

F. J. Foakes-Jackson. (1927). Peter: Prince of Apostles, A Study in the History and Tradition of Christianity. New York: George H. Doran. (Original work published 1927)

Mark A. Chancey. (2002). The Myth of a Gentile Galilee The Population of Galilee and New Testament Studies. Cambridge, UK: Cambridge University Press. (Original work published 2002)

Maurice Casey. (1999). Aramaic Sources of Mark's Gospel. Cambridge, UK: Cambridge University Press. (Original work published 1999)

(http://www.pbs.org/wgbh/pages/frontline/shows/religion/jesus/tikkun.html, April 27, 2011).

(http://www.pbs.org/wgbh/pages/frontline/shows/reli
gion/jesus/tikkun.html, April 29, 2011).

(http://www.michaelturton.com/Mark/GMark_intro.ht
ml, April 29, 2011)